AF270620

Play-Doh

by Grace Hansen

Abdo Kids Jumbo is an Imprint of Abdo Kids
abdobooks.com

abdobooks.com

Published by Abdo Kids, a division of ABDO, P.O. Box 398166, Minneapolis, Minnesota 55439.
Copyright © 2023 by Abdo Consulting Group, Inc. International copyrights reserved in all countries.
No part of this book may be reproduced in any form without written permission from the publisher.
Abdo Kids Jumbo™ is a trademark and logo of Abdo Kids.

Printed in China.

102022

012023

Photo Credits: Alamy, Getty Images, Shutterstock, ©Steve Carlin Papers, di_05811, The Dolph Briscoe
Center for American History, The University of Texas at Austin, p7,
©Courtesy of The Strong, Rochester, New York, p15 p19

Production Contributors: Teddy Borth, Jennie Forsberg, Grace Hansen
Design Contributors: Candice Keimig, Pakou Moua

Library of Congress Control Number: 2022937181

Publisher's Cataloging-in-Publication Data

Names: Hansen, Grace, author.

Title: Play-Doh / by Grace Hansen

Description: Minneapolis, Minnesota : Abdo Kids, 2023 | Series: Toy mania! | Includes online resources and
index.

Identifiers: ISBN 9781098264291 (lib. bdg.) | ISBN 9781098264857 (ebook) | ISBN 9781098265137
(Read-to-Me ebook)

Subjects: LCSH: Play-Doh (Toy)--Juvenile literature. | Polymer clay craft--Juvenile literature. | Toys--
Juvenile literature. | Hasbro, Inc.--Juvenile literature.

Classification: DDC 731.2--dc23

Table of Contents

Play-Doh

Few people know that Play-Doh began as a cleaning product. Today, Play-Doh is used for good, clean fun!

A Flexible Product

Joseph McVicker was born on September 9, 1930, in Cincinnati, Ohio. His family owned a company called Kutol Products. The company made soaps and other cleaning supplies.

Cincinnati, Ohio
Joseph McVicker

In the 1930s, homes were heated with **coal**. The smoke left **soot** on people's walls. Kutol Wall Cleaner was just the thing to help. It was thick like clay and didn't damage wallpaper.

blue
coal

In the 1940s, new fuels replaced **coal** to heat homes. They did not leave **soot** on the walls. Joseph needed a new idea. His sister-in-law, Kay, was a schoolteacher. Her students used Kutol Wall Cleaner to make art projects.

Joseph decided to sell the product to schools. But first, he made some changes to the dough to make it smell better. Now, it needed a name. Kay's husband came up with Play-Doh!

Play-Doh

Fun of All Shapes and Sizes!

In 1955, Joseph introduced Play-Doh at a school supply convention. A department store decided to sell it as a toy. Play-Doh was popular both at home and in the classroom.

make ...
BUILDING PROJECTS
RAILROAD IDEAS
GIFTS AND JEWELRY
...make hundreds of exciting modeling projects with your FUN FACTORY!
The Original Play-Doh
ideal gift for year 'round family fun!
Play-Doh Modeling Compound
The Original Play-Doh MODELING COMPOUND
CLEAN · NON-TOXIC
III
FUN FACTORY
TOY EXTRUDER
BY THE MAKERS OF
Play-Doh MODELING COMPOUND

In 1956, the McVickers founded Rainbow Crafts Company, Inc. A year later, the company introduced Play-Doh in red, blue, and yellow. Today, there are many colors to choose from!

In 1957, Joseph hired Dr. Tien Liu

to improve the Play-Doh product.

Dr. Liu's changes helped the

dough last longer. It could now

be played with many times.

The Original
Play-Doh®
Pat. No. 3,167,440   BRAND
MODELING COMPOUND
CLEAN • NON-TOXIC
TM

Play-Doh is still popular

today. With a little time and

imagination, Play-Doh can

become anything kids want it

to be!

More Facts

- Play-Doh was **inducted** into the National Toy Hall of Fame in 1998.

- For Play-Doh's 50th anniversary in 2006, Hasbro released the Play-Doh fragrance!

- Play-Doh is mainly made up of water, a starch-based binder, and salt. It is non-toxic and comes in 60 colors. There is also Sparkle and Confetti Play-Doh!

Glossary

coal – a hard black or dark brown substance that is found in the earth and burned as fuel.

convention – a formal meeting or gathering where people discuss shared interests.

department store – a large store with separate departments, each selling a certain type of goods.

imagination – the act or power of the mind to form a thought, picture, or image of something.

inducted – brought in as a member.

soot – a fine, black powder made during burning.

Index

Abdo Kids ONLINE
FREE! ONLINE MULTIMEDIA RESOURCES

Visit **abdokids.com** to access crafts, games, videos, and more!